It was in Dallas, Texas, 20(Thompson. She and her training program that I was facilitating for her company.

As the session got underway one of the participants really shined in the group. It was her smile and unique interest in others. She seldom talked about herself. It was her genuine "Zeal 4 Life" that got my attention. Sue shared with me her cancer journey and that she managed to survive when the outlook was grim. It appeared her inspirational and human attitude contributed greatly to her success. She became determined to help others focus on what's positive and appreciate everything they have and to celebrate life. It was in her survivor mindset that she found the power to broadcast her healing attitudes and beliefs to others. It reminds me of the quote by Andrew Carnegie "Whatever the mind can conceive, and believe, it can achieve."

I have been reading Sue's *Good Monday Morning* messages every week for eight years and they are at the top of my priority list as "required reading" every Monday morning. It is a wonderful way to start the week, upbeat, energetic and ready to take on anything. They are highly inspirational, down to earth, and fun. I share the weekly message with family and friends. They too have found Sue's words to be very appropriate and helpful in getting their week off to a positive start.

P. Maw
Management Consultant
Vancouver, BC

"After hiring Sue in the early 80's as a sales executive in the publishing industry, she became one of the most powerful influences in my life.

Still one of the best 'door openers' in the business, her positive outlook is captivating and her laugh is contagious. Her faith, energy and gratitude has enabled her to overcome adversities, including cancer. She's a fighter, a believer, and a classic example of someone who's manifested their own destiny.

Over time, Sue helped me transform my life, encouraging me to 'let go' and 'open my heart'. And I realize how blessed I am to know her. She truly lives life with passion, and continues to inspire me with her *Good Monday Morning* emails."

PK Dailey
Director Print Production
Dieste, Inc

"Sue's story is not about surviving, it is about LIVING! Sue honestly loves life and is passionate about getting the most out of it she can, every day. Sue has an incredible story of overcoming an incurable disease in spite of the medical odds against her. Hearing her story about her unwavering faith in God and in life, will renew your hope and inspire you to be stronger and more determined to live YOUR life with passion!"

Dianne N.
Frisco, Texas

"Sue's *Good Monday Morning* messages are greatly appreciated and a superb way to get an early lift to the week. They always inspire magical moments and get me thinking in a new direction. I read them carefully and forward them to the appropriate people. I can't thank you enough."

Peter M.
Vancouver, B.C.

"It's not Monday without Sue's words of encouragement to start my week! The morsels of wisdom are enjoyed by me and shared with others. When I run across someone that needs a boost, I forward them Sue's message. I am so very appreciative."

John M.
Toledo, Ohio

"Passionate, tenacious, purposeful, dynamic, positive, dependable, cheerful, enthusiastic, warm, fun, unstoppable, tireless, energetic, determined…these are a few of my favorite words that describe Sue Thompson. What a winner!"

Leslie M.
Dallas, Texas

"I met Sue 16 years ago through our businesses. Over the years we have bumped in to each other from time to time and I want her to know what an inspiration she is to me. Actually, she is a pivotal person in my life and someone who comes to mind often.

I remember seeing her at a convention many years ago in Amelia Island, Florida. I was newly engaged and so excited about my ring and what the future held. Sue was very ill and so very weak. Yet, she carried on with a sparkle of light. I had been going through some tough times with the owners of my company and she inspired me to just be myself. Not to worry what others thought or said about me.

We had a quick chat about discovering who your true friends are in bad times. My bad times were absolutely nothing compared to the illness she was battling. I admired her spunk and spirit to live and carry on. That quick conversation meant the world to me.

When the convention was over, I remember boarding the bus to the airport very, very early in the morning. Sue was seated right in front of me on the bus. I remember thinking how she amazed me. She had a good friend with her to lean on, help her carry her luggage, and help her all the way with whatever she needed. I was watching in awe! Deep down I was so afraid that I was not going to see her again. To my surprise and wonder, a few years later I saw her at a luncheon. She looked fabulous and had the biggest smile on her face and a twinkle in her eyes. I was over the moon excited seeing her.

Whenever I found myself in a tough spot in life or trying to work through something, I always thought of Sue and her sparkle! Because of her, I never allowed myself to curl up in the corner and give up.

I think the absolute world of Sue and her accomplishments. She has always been someone that lights up a room and I am so honored and happy to call her friend.

I know she has inspired me as well as many, many people and will continue to do so! I love her so much!"

N. Rowe
Frisco, TX

HEALTH · OPTIMISM · PASSION · ENTHUSIASM

TALKS

INSPIRATION TO LIVE YOUR LIFE WITH PASSION

SUE S. THOMPSON

H.O.P.E. Talks: Inspiration to Live Your Life With Passion
Copyright © 2013 by Sue S. Thompson (Zeal 4 Life). All rights reserved.
First Print Edition: July 2013
Zeal 4 Life Publishing Company
San Antonio, TX
www.zeal4life.net

ISBN 13 – Print Edition: 978-1-4929-7519-9
ISBN 13 – Kindle Edition 978-1-62480-088-7
ISBN 13 – E-Pub Edition 978-1-62480-089-4

"Hope sees the invisible, feels the intangible, and achieves the impossible."

—Anonymous

TABLE OF CONTENTS

What People Are Saying… i

In Loving Gratitude xix

In Loving Memory xx

Larger Than Life xxi

A Moment Of H.O.P.E. xxiii

Chapter 1 27

   H.ealth **29**

   Serving 31

   What Is Your "Why" 32

   Pursuit Of Wealth 33

   Cancel, Cancel, Cancel 34

   Happiness 35

   Three Things 36

   Be Grounded In Your Life 37

   I Like You 38

   Dan's Laughter 39

   Something To Ponder 40

   Wellness 41

   Why Am I Blessed? 42

   Language Is Vibration 43

   Gift Of Sight 44

   It's Up To You 45

Living Life In A Hurry......................46
You Are Worth It.............................47
Think Of The Future........................48
Life Is Not Measured.......................49
Prosperity....................................50
Uncommonly Unique......................51
Your Choice..................................52
Your To Do List.............................53
Chapter 2.....................................55
O.ptimism.................................**57**
Each Day......................................58
Living With Richness......................59
What Are You Thinking..................60
Why Not?.....................................61
Your Potential...............................62
Stuck..63
Starting Today..............................64
Do You Have A Dream?..................65
Keep Your Feet Moving...................66
Passionate About My Life...............67
Emmit Smith Says.........................68
Remember....................................69
A New Life...................................70
Family Time Is Special...................71
Check Your Price Tag.....................72
Create The Life You Want...............73
Now..74
Life's Little Instructions.................75
Beginning Today...........................77
Keep Everything In Perspective.......79
Staying Positive Through Home Robbery.......80

Success 81
What Is Your Vision? 82
H.O.P.E. Is The Anchor 83
Chapter 3 85
P.assion **87**
Life Is An Echo 88
Be Happy 89
For Anyone Who Has A Dream 90
The Best Is Yet To Come 92
A Dream Without A Plan Is Only A Wish 93
Happiness Can Be So Simple 94
Completing Things 95
Life Map 97
Your Passionate Purpose 98
Isn't Life Just Grand 99
Passion 100
The Power Is Yours 101
Aspire 102
A Good Enough Reason 103
Life's Gift 104
Best Day Ever 105
Where Are You? 107
Attitude vs Talent 108
Mama's Inspiring Words 109
Commitment 110
Inner Conversations 111
Four Things For Sure 112
Just Do It 113
Reason, Purpose, Massive Action Plan 114

Chapter 4 115

E.nthusiasm **117**

Habits 118

Count Your Blessings 119

Boiling Point 120

What Is Your Word? 121

Say What You Mean 122

Do You? 123

Four Kinds of People 124

Today's Treasures 126

Step Out 127

Attitude Is Everything 128

Make Your Shots 129

Begin 130

Happiness Is Your Choice 131

Honor The Beginning 132

Possibilities vs Inadequacies 134

I Can Do Anything 135

The Wait Is Over 136

Isn't Life Full Of Surprises? 137

Explore New Possibilities 138

Never Let Go Of Hope 139

Dream Big Dreams 140

7 Rules To Live By 141

Remember 143

Isn't Life Awesome? 144

End Notes 145

About Sue Thompson 146

Contact The Author 148

My Own Inspirations 149

Dedicated to my "Zeals 4 Life"

My two loving sons, **Chip and Brooks Thompson**,
who have been the most blessed gifts God
has given me. They are beautiful souls and
have not only brought me many years of love and
happiness, but have stood by my side
during very scary times.
And they have given me #1 on my bucket list—
five beautiful granddaughters!

My devoted sister, **Jan Zuehlke**,
Who has never, ever left my side, during
good or challenging times.
She has always been there to love, support and take care of
me. She is not only my little sister, but my best friend!

Left to right: Brooke, Addison, Ryan

Peyton, & Sidney

My 5 precious granddaughters—*my reasons for living*—
They bring me such joy and happiness and I am so
blessed that God allowed me to live a healthy life to
be their Mamaw! I love each of them
to the moon and back!

IN LOVING GRATITUDE

To those who never gave up on me or this book becoming a reality. They had the belief in me before I did. Their love, support and encouragement gave me the confirmation that I needed to write this book!

I thank you and love you so very much...

My wonderful sister and best friend, Jan Zuehlke and brother-in-law, Zeke for their continuous belief in me,

My loving nieces' Lara Zuehlke and Jana Z. Bennette,

My beautiful daughter-in-law, Michelle Thompson,

My friend, Eric Meyer who called me daily to confirm I was working "on my book,"

My life-long friend, Kay Cunningham and Paul for giving me a condo on the beach at South Padre to compile this book!

IN LOVING MEMORY

My Mama and Daddy, Faye and Jim Sellers

My beautiful cousin, Resa Murphy

My Nantie, Flo Rutter

My "other" parents, Reete and Tom Holmes

LARGER THAN LIFE

Have you ever met one of those people who just bring inexplicable joy? Who lights up the room and leaves an impression so that you never forget them?

Sue Thompson is one of those people.

As a child, Sue would blow into town with sacks of candy and bubble gum cigars. For my brother, sister, and me growing up in a small Texas town, Sue was larger than life itself. Her energy and enthusiasm and everything about her was infectious. And though we didn't live near "crazy Aunt Sue," as we affectionately called her, Sue and I shared a deep, soul connection from the get-go.

So on that Tuesday in 1999 when my mom called me at work to tell me "crazy Aunt Sue" had been diagnosed with a blood cancer, I was beyond devastated. I was crushed and heartbroken. Tears sprang to my eyes and didn't stop crying until I talked to Sue later that day.

"Lara, I'm not going to die so just stop crying. It's going to be okay." Sue told me over the phone. Here she was the one diagnosed with cancer and she was consoling me!

Watching Sue navigate that journey with cancer, not to mention the many twists and turns of her life, hasn't only inspired me, it's inspired everyone who knows Sue or even hears of her. Over the years, I've had friends who've met her once, twenty years ago, and still ask about her to this day.

It is that same infectious energy and enthusiasm for life that you will discover through these pages of *H.O.P.E. Talks*. Where so many books dish up platitudes that make you feel good, what you'll find in this collection is so much more. For the words that line these pages come from a woman who by every measure should have given up on life a long time ago, but she didn't.

Whether it's the fact that she's a feisty redhead or the fact that she's just plain stubborn, Sue defied the odds and today lives, breathes, and embodies the principles and ideas she shares in *H.O.P.E. Talks*.

May Sue's words not only inspire you, may they move you to action to live in such a way that you inspire others as well.

Lara Zuehlke

A MOMENT OF H.O.P.E.

It was a beautiful, sunny day in the spring of 2000, almost one year from the day I was diagnosed with Multiple Myeloma. Driving along my usual route down Highway 105, I passed alongside a calm, blue lake where the sun danced across the water like sparklers on the Fourth of July. Deep in conversation with God, I asked to please reveal if, and how, I was to take all I had experienced and share it through inspiring talks.

At the time, I was the manager of a large real estate office and my agents were encouraging me to share my story. It didn't seem to me a particularly inspiring one—for it was my life. I was just doing what anyone does when faced with a life-threatening challenge: Keep moving forward the best way you know how, one foot in front of another. Though the day I received the diagnosis, I made the conscious decision to heal my body the way I felt God intended–naturally.

The real estate agents at my office were relentless (as agents can sometimes be). So every day, at least one person would tell me that others needed to hear about how I was responding to this health challenge in such a strong and positive way. To me, this was just another hurdle I had to jump and knew in my heart that God would give me the strength to overcome it!

As I glanced across the lake that warm spring day, I knew (in that place you just *know*) that God would provide the sign I needed and show me what to do to help others.

As I quietly drove along, in a split second, I saw the answer.

In the brilliant blue sky sat large white clouds thick as shaving cream. As the mound of clouds began to disperse, the letters H.O.P.E. appeared. Needless to say, I almost ran the car off the road!

Overwhelmed with the amazing clarity of this message, I pulled the car over to the shoulder where I sat and stared for several minutes at this vision. Then I immediately called my sister, hysterically telling her about this miracle.

"But Jan, what does this mean? What does H.O.P.E. stand for? Why are there dots after each letter?" I asked excitedly.

In her very calm way, my sister replied, "Sue, calm down. That is obviously the name of your talks and God will reveal why there are periods after each letter when the time is right."

When I finally arrived home, I walked through the door and set my purse on the chair. In a flash of a moment, with the same clarity and power God had spoken to me in the doctor's office the day I was told I had an "incurable cancer," I heard this message:

"H.ealth, O.ptimism, P.assion, E.nthusiasm. That is what your inspirational talks are about. Now go share your story and make a difference to help others!"

And so a year later I began my journey of *H.O.P.E. Talks.* It was 7 A.M. on a Monday morning in 2001 and like most early mornings I was up checking email. I came across one message that really spoke to me, so I forwarded it to a friend. When I hit the "send" button, a box popped up alerting me there was no subject. I leaned back in my chair and thought, hmm, what is the subject for this message?

God spoke to me again and said in a clear, humorous voice: "*Good Monday Morning—that works, and by the way, you should do this each week to inspire others.*"

Oh sure, I thought, how will I do that?

But of course, the way was revealed. So every Monday morning since 2001, I have sent a *Good Monday Morning* message to hundreds of people, inspiring them each week with the message that wants to be shared. It is from those many years of *Good Monday Morning* messages, along with the insight I've gained along my journey of healing, that this book came to life.

This book is designed to be read in the way each Monday message was intended: To provide you short doses of inspiration to encourage you through life's downs and celebrate with you all of the ups. May these words uplift and encourage you to keep moving forward each day knowing that every moment is a gift.

And above all, may they inspire you to live with passion!

Many Blessings and May You Always Have Faith,

Sue

CHAPTER 1

H. EALTH
O. PTIMISM
P. ASSION
E. NTHUSIASM

HEALTH

My entire life I have been healthy, never worrying about weight, what I ate, pimples, sleep or anything that remotely resembled taking care of myself. I just hurried through each day burning the candle at both ends, so to speak. I was a bundle of energy.

The truth is I took my health for granted. I didn't respect my body or understand how to live a life of balance.

Then one day when the rug was pulled out from under me, I quickly learned how to cherish and nourish the temple that God gifted me.

Life is not about how to survive in a storm, but how to dance in the rain.

—Author Unknown

A remarkable journey in my life began August 31, 1999. I was diagnosed with Multiple Myeloma, a blood related cancer. By the grace of God, a strong determination and a positive attitude, I defied all medical journals and doctor's reports and today celebrate my life now in total wellness!

I urge you to wake up each morning with "an attitude of gratitude," laugh your way through each day, think only positive thoughts because they do become your reality, choose to celebrate and savor each moment you have, live a magical life and always believe in miracles...

Something special will come your way when you do!

—*Sue*

H.ealth

SERVING

Michelle, my daughter in law is always telling Ryan and Brooke that the player who serves the best very seldom loses. Isn't life just like a tennis game?

When we live with an attitude of gratitude and servitude, our life flows in a positive, beautiful way…and we win our serve!

We all know what a crisis we are in today—too much cancer, diabetes, obesity and general poor health. How can we be of "service" to change this way of life? There are answers to heal ourselves naturally, the way it is intended.

Live your life with passion, thinking only positive thoughts because they do become your reality.

H.ealth

WHAT IS YOUR "WHY"

What gets you up in the morning?

What drives you each day?

Do you know your "Why" for living?

What lights a fire within you?

If you aren't clear on these questions, I invite you to take some quiet time and come up with the answers. They are there—just not always so clear. If it creates emotion within you, you are getting close to finding out your why!

I became very clear of my Why the day I was diagnosed with cancer. I knew I had to live because the #1 thing on my Bucket List was to be a grandma. I prayed long and hard to God asking Him to please not only let me live, but to live a long and healthy life so that I could have quality, fun, loving times with grandkids. He blessed me by answering that prayer and today I am Mamaw to my five beautiful gifts and it motivates me each day to live with a positive attitude and a heart of gratitude!

Life is intended to be lived to the fullest, filling your days with fun, love, laughter, peace and satisfaction and always keeping your faith. Go for it—live your life with passion every second of every day.

H.ealth

PURSUIT OF WEALTH

If your pursuit of wealth causes you to sacrifice any aspect of your health, your priorities are turned around. Your physical condition is your compass; it will tell you if you are headed in the right direction or if you're going astray. It's not your checkbook, but *you* who is counted on to be there for the people in your world are the checkbook. Be far-sighted. Weigh the differences. Think of the prices you pay.

In my past, I was the perfect example of the word "workaholic." I worked very long hours, didn't nourish or cherish my body and burned the candle at both ends, until 1999 when I hit the wall. My body was tired and unhealthy. It took being diagnosed with cancer for me to hear the message loud and clear—*SLOW DOWN, TAKE CARE OF YOURSELF!*

H.ealth

CANCEL, CANCEL, CANCEL

Our life is shaped by our mind; we become what we think.

Joy follows a pure thought like a shadow that never leaves.

—Author Unknown

One of the most profound lessons I have learned on my journey in life is that it is imperative that we think positive thoughts and speak positive words because they absolutely do become our reality!

Every time a negative thought or word approaches me, I immediately say "cancel, cancel, cancel" and amazingly enough it just vanishes into thin air. I invite you to try this and see if it makes a difference in your life.

H.ealth

HAPPINESS

Don't let your happiness be held hostage. It is always yours to choose, to live, to experience.

You don't need anyone else's permission to be happy. Your life is magnificent not because someone says it is, but because you choose it to be.

Every day you will fulfill your most sincere expectations if you expect to be happy.

Simply choose and your circumstances start to line up around that happiness.

It is your choice. Choose it any time you wish.

H.ealth

THREE THINGS

In my opinion, in order to succeed in life you need three things...

A *"Wish" Bone*—allow yourself to dream big and remember that a wish without a plan simply remains a wish!

A *"Back" Bone*—it's all about taking ownership of your life because what others think of you does not determine who you are. In your heart, you know who that special person is so why not live the life you deserve!

A *"Funny" Bone*—Laughter is the cure for all things that ail you. Life is to be lived to the fullest every single day because we must always remember that "this ain't no dress rehearsal"—we don't get "do overs!" Life is a journey, not a destination, so why not allow yours to be positive and fun while manifesting the life you want?

I am living proof that when you take ownership of your life, visualize your dream and create a plan, it will become reality.

Being in severe pain in the early days of the cancer challenge, I watched Dr. Doolittle and laughed until I cried, which is proof that laughter is the cure for all things!

I can promise you this—I will sing my song while still on earth and make it known how grateful I am to be alive to sing my song! Live your life with passion and have no regrets!

H.ealth

BE GROUNDED IN YOUR LIFE

Create a vision of all the places and people you have interacted with that have affected and blessed you in your life's path...

By celebrating what is right in your world, you create good in what's wrong in your world!

Live your life from the "inside out"—then you become grounded in your reality and set the truth free of what a beautiful gift you are to this world.

Sometimes we discover that our hardest challenges in life create our most positive life lessons. I have experienced many in my life's journey and have reached the realization that I wouldn't change a single experience in my life, no matter how tough or sad it was at the time. I remained grounded and chose to celebrate the good times.

H.ealth

I LIKE YOU

When I was diagnosed with the "incurable cancer" in 1999, I had no grandchildren and that was definitely #1 on my "bucket list!" Six weeks after the diagnosis, we found out my first grandchild was on the way. What an awesome gift that news was to me. She was born on May 18 and named Ryan Michelle. We have made so many wonderful memories together over the years.

Our family went to "Disney on Ice." Walking to the parking lot after the show, Ryan, and I were arm and arm, giggling and laughing. She looked me straight in the eyes and said "Mamaw, I really like you so much." We are always saying "I Love You," but to have your granddaughter say she "likes" you is extremely special!

I told her, through teary eyes, that was a very special thing to say. You can love someone and not like them very much. I hadn't really thought of that concept in a long time. So, my "aha" to share with you is to take time to tell someone special you like them. It is a completely different feeling! And, if you don't like them, then I invite you to find something about them you do like that will outweigh what you don't.

H.ealth

DAN'S LAUGHTER

Everyday life is so full of unexpected and expected situations. I spent a week with friends, my son and beautiful granddaughters, loving every second of each day and living in gratitude for my blessings.

Then on Sunday morning I received a devastating call that one of my dearest and oldest friends (years being friends, not age) lost his battle with cancer. When we hear this news we feel so helpless and empty inside. Immediately all the awesome memories you have shared come rushing into your heart. You feel happy, then the reality hits again and you feel such sadness in your heart. We know that none of us is getting out of here alive, right? But it still hurts so much when you lose someone you love.

Dan was always laughing and making others laugh…I started reading a new book on Sunday night and there was a chapter on "Laughter"—I thought of him while reading and tears of wonderful memories along with tears of sadness hit the pages. There is a quote in the book that I want to share with you… and invite you to laugh each day of your life and live it with passion and gratitude.

Laughter is such good medicine for our soul…unfortunately; our world is desperately in need of more such medicine.

To Dan, who was like my brother—May you rest in peace and know how much you are loved!

H.ealth

SOMETHING TO PONDER

I remember hearing Zig Ziglar many times talk about money wasn't everything but ranked up there with oxygen. I totally agree with him because we must have money to survive in this world.

However, there are many who feel that money is the most important thing in their lives and that they could not live without it. This is not true.

There is something far more important and precious for us without which we could not live. What is that? It is our breath! Our breath is the most precious substance in our lives, and yet we totally take it for granted when we exhale that our next breath will be there. So if we have been given enough breath to last as long as we live, can we not trust that everything else we need will also be supplied?

So as Zig Ziglar stated—it just ranks right up there with oxygen, not more important than!

H.ealth

WELLNESS

Wellness is the dance of life that celebrates infinite and eternal harmony. It is the dynamic activity of caring for your body as the home for your soul; the enriching quality of striving to fulfill your highest potential; and the elevating state of filling your life with love. To achieve wellness is to attain the point of balance where the energies of body, mind, and spirit are so finely attuned to each other that distinctions between them fade away.

Wellness was certainly not a word I related to until August 1999. Today I understand the importance of being in balance and how that creates harmony of body, mind and spirit. After all, it is our life to live and make our own choices —I invite you to choose wisely!

H.ealth

WHY AM I BLESSED?

There are so many things we can do to live an abundant life. Here are a few questions to think about that could create a special day not only for you, but for those around you.

What can I do to surprise a loved one to make them smile?

Who do I love in my life? Why do I love them? How will I show them?

How will I exercise today to increase my energy and make me stronger?

Which tape will I listen to today to boost my earning power?

What book can I read tonight to enlighten and inspire me?

How will I convert a current customer to a Raving Fan today?

What successes and moments did I have today to write in my Gratitude Journal?

What fruit can I eat today to give me quick energy and cleanse me?

Did I nourish my body today with good nutritional foods?

Will today's activities keep me on track to live my dreams?

What will I do to make a difference in someone's life today?

I am always reminding myself that we don't get "do overs" in our life's journey. All we have to embrace is the moment we are in.

H.ealth

LANGUAGE IS VIBRATION

Would you agree with me that every word uttered and every thought that passes through us is an affirmation? Our language and thoughts shape energy into matter. If what we say matters to us, it ultimately turns into physical manifestation.

All language is vibration. Vibration includes sound and light. Language is the process of Spirit (breath, inspiration) becoming reality! Words spoken with specificity and feeling equals manifestation!

> *By your words you shall be justified and by your words you shall be condemned.* Matthew 12:37 [1]

When I went through the challenging journey years ago, I became very aware of my spoken words and my thoughts. Every time a negative one appeared, I immediately said "cancel, cancel, cancel." It works! I have discovered another way to say that, which I am choosing to say now: "In the past, cancel, clear."

I invite you to become aware of your language and your thoughts. Choose only the positive ones to create your reality...so every time you choose to neutralize the power of a statement or thought and cancel its creative energy, say "In the past, cancel, clear" or say "cancel, cancel, cancel." A whole new world will be your reality!

H.ealth

GIFT OF SIGHT

Do you hurry through each day of your life in a rush? Life can be such a hassle each day to just get the things done on your list that we sometimes forget to slow down, take a good, deep breath and be grateful for the gifts we have. Unintentionally, we take so much for granted!

A friend sent me an email this morning on "color." As I watched the beautiful slide show, I realized that I take my sight for granted. I know I will see color in everything. How sad it would be if I couldn't see and had to miss all the beauty God has surrounded me with.

So, I ask you to slow down this week, take a deep breath, and not only enjoy the beauty all around you, but live your life with an "attitude of gratitude."

H.ealth

IT'S UP TO YOU

This life is the only one you are given.

Look for opportunities to grow, and never be discouraged in your efforts to do so.

Replace your weaknesses with strengths.

Take life's broken pieces and re-create your dreams.

Never measure the future by the past; let yesterday become a memory and tomorrow a promise.

It is up to you to stay happy and healthy. This is your life – take ownership of it. Start today to live in WELLNESS and "balance." I love life and am very blessed to have been given the gift again!

H.ealth

LIVING LIFE IN A HURRY

Why do we live our lives in such a hurry? Every day seems to pass quicker than the one before. We need to stop, enjoy and savor every moment we are given each and every day.

Just think how awesome it would be if we truly kept our bodies in a healthy, balanced state. It is a possibility—we just have to make that decision for it to be our reality.

This reminds me of when I was a junior in high school and my Mama gave me a candle for my birthday. It was Holly Hobby smelling flowers in a garden and it said "Stop and Smell the Roses." I thought that was the strangest gift I had ever received. She looked at me and said "Sister, one day this will make sense to you." Sure! I thought. Well, as it is that Mothers are usually right, it all came to light the day I was diagnosed with the "incurable cancer." I realized at that moment that life is brief and very fragile, we need to slow down and smell the roses and savor and enjoy every moment we are given in this gift of life!

H.ealth

YOU ARE WORTH IT

Take today to just stop for a little while and listen. Re-acquaint yourself with the beautiful, peaceful, intuitive person you are inside.

The oh-so-urgent concerns of the world can wait for a little bit. Take some time to listen to the wisdom that speaks softly but profoundly at the center of your being.

Remember what you have forgotten, and discover what you never before realized you knew. Don't be so busy chasing success that you lose touch with why you're doing it.

Quiet your thoughts and know the things that you can know without thinking. Give your dreams and your highest visions the chance to catch up with you.

Listen, without the need to interrupt or judge, or interject your thoughts. Just listen, and know.

Take some quiet, peaceful time to listen, to accept the wisdom, and to know. Know you are a very special gift and be grateful every day for your life! You are worth it!!

H.ealth

THINK OF THE FUTURE

I heard my precious niece, Lara, say *"don't think of the future as something in front of you—think of the future as something inside you waiting to be discovered."* That touched me to my very soul!

For some reason it reminded me of a very special, yet terrifying time that the future was what I held on to. On November 12, 2009, my fifth granddaughter, Sidney Lane, was born. Her lungs were not formed fully and she was in the NICU for the next few days. It was horrifying seeing God's precious little gift with tubes in her and so helpless. They allowed me to hold her so I would assure her that she would live and be a beautiful, feisty girl and hold a very special place in her Mamaw's heart. God answered our prayers and today she is definitely that and more.

Life is for Laughing, Loving, Forgiving
and Living with Passion.

H.ealth

LIFE IS NOT MEASURED

Life can bring such amazing surprises...and from my life's experiences, I have learned to accept each day with celebration and know in my heart it is exactly as it should be. Even when we are challenged, we must remember that!

So I invite you to savor each and every moment of life you have been given and only focus on the positive and let the negative go. Celebrate with love, fun and laughter.

> *"Life is not measured by the number of breaths you take but by the moments that take your breath away."*

—Author Unknown

Make today and everyday an extra special day in your beautiful life!

H.ealth

PROSPERITY

As we live our lives each day, do we truly know that we are living a prosperous one?

Something to think about...instead of creating a "bucket" list, why not create a "living" list? Why not live your life each day to the fullest and create a reality of your dreams? I am living proof that manifestation works if you truly believe in your heart that it does and keep your faith that it will become reality.

There are 3 parts to manifestation:

(1) Thinking;

(2) Feeling;

(3) Picturing.

Think what you desire, feel it to your very core and then picture it as if you are in the moment. Your life will forever be altered...

Don't attempt to "set" it right—"see" it right.

H.ealth

UNCOMMONLY UNIQUE

Don't dull your life by missing this point:

You are more than statistical chance, more than a marriage of heredity and society, more than a confluence of inherited chromosomes and childhood trauma. More than a walking weather vane whipped about by the cold winds of fate.

–Author Unknown

Thanks to God you have been sculpted from nothing into something.

Your being born was no accident. You were created to do something special and make a difference in all who cross your path.

What our minds can believe, we can achieve.

H.ealth

YOUR CHOICE

You can choose your perspective, you can choose your outlook, and you can choose your attitude. The moment you make the choice, whatever you choose is yours. It doesn't matter what you have experienced or how you have felt for the last hour, or month, or year. In the next moment you can be feeling precisely the way you choose to feel. I believe that the most powerful gift God gives us is our mind.

You are just a moment away from being the most highly motivated person you know. Choose to be that person. Your greatest success begins right now. Choose the positive, empowering perspective that will bring it to life!

H.ealth

YOUR TO DO LIST

Is your "to do" list keeping you up at night?

Do you feel like your stress is off the charts?

Here is something that will make you stop and think:

Did you know that your stress is really your choice?

That's a liberating concept because if stress is a choice, you can choose not to have it. To experience a simplified life, we first have to learn to slow down long enough to see through all the clutter. We need to realize that we are powerful magnets and have the power to create our reality! Do not wait until a crisis appears and gives you no choice, as I did. Know that you can own your reality so that no crisis ever approaches you.

Always remember to think and speak positively because they do become your reality.

CHAPTER 2

H. EALTH
O. PTIMISM
P. ASSION
E. NTHUSIASM

OPTIMISM

From birth I've always looked on the bright side of life's ventures. I believe in good over evil!

Life is an adventure—it's not about the destination, but the journey. Each day presents new experiences, as well as challenges. Isn't that how we learn our life lessons that create the map for our journey?

I am living proof that positive words and thoughts create our reality.

We can manifest anything our heart desires if we want it enough!

Life is a journey—wake up expecting miracle.

—Sue

O.ptimism

EACH DAY

Each day is like a work of art that's yet to be designed, an empty canvas waiting for the dreams that fill your mind...

Your talents and your strengths are like the colors you can use to paint the pictures of your life in any way you choose.

—Author Unknown

Imagine a portrait of your life...

Visualize the scenery, the colors, the characters.

God allowed me to slow down and create my canvas of a life filled with fun, love, laughter and good health and be Mamaw to five incredible, beautiful girls.

O.ptimism

LIVING WITH RICHNESS

Realize the power you have to make a difference. Think of the value that you can now create. There is no end to the love you can give. There is no limit to the joy you can share.

Your vision, your imagination and your intentions point the way forward. Your thoughts and actions can bring the fulfillment you seek.

Open yourself to the goodness and to the opportunities that are yours right now. There is much for which to be thankful, and there are countless ways to express and fulfill your purpose.

Get busy living this day with richness and your own special meaning. Feel the unique joy of this moment, and carry it ever forward.

—Ralph Marston [2]

An ounce of ACTION is better than a ton of THEORY

Make a decision today to live your life in richness!

Short, sweet, simple and so true!

O.ptimism

WHAT ARE YOU THINKING

Positive thinking empowers much more than your thoughts—it creates your reality!

Negative thinking can dismantle every part of your life!

You always have a choice of what to think. When making that choice, always remember each thought has great power that continues long after the thought has passed from your consciousness.

Have you ever wanted something so much you would do anything (within reason and legally) to get it?

I recall a company I was partnered with offered an all-expense paid trip to Cancun for a company convention. The volume to qualify was more than I had produced in any given time period—we had 3 months to produce the volume. I was determined to go on that trip so I began visualizing how it would be to win it!

I could see me on the airplane to Cancun, walking on the beach, hearing the sea gulls, feeling and smelling the salt air, the crashing of the waves on the shoreline and me walking across the stage with hundreds watching me accept an award. AND within two months I qualified! Never, ever doubt the power of your mind and that what you think and what you speak does become your reality!

O.ptimism

WHY NOT?

What is your dream?

What are your goals?

Have you slowed down long enough to know what these are?

Have you written them down?

Do you truly believe you can have them?

Do you believe you deserve them?

Well, You Do!! Why Not??

Go for it—this time all the way—don't let anything stop you!!!

Wake up each morning with an attitude of gratitude and savor and enjoy each moment of your incredible life...live your life with passion!

O.ptimism

YOUR POTENTIAL

There is no limit to your potential.

For there is no limit to what you can imagine, and whatever you can imagine, you can bring into your life.

There are always very real hurdles, but in some way or another, you can get yourself over every one of them.

Focus your imagination on the positive possibilities, and focus your efforts on making them real.

Feel the unique potential that is your life. Give your own special beauty to the world.

Live For Today—Celebrate Your Life!

O.*ptimism*

STUCK

For the first time in years, I am "stuck" on what to share this week. I have been so blessed over the last few days that I'm in awe of how amazing life can be! Isn't it interesting that when our life is on track that we somehow want to ignore that and do our best to find the wrong things? Crazy, isn't it? Why not let go and let God and enjoy and savor the good blessings we are receiving? I am so excited about the path my life is on and am so grateful that I am in perfect health, have quality time with my granddaughters in San Antonio, missing my granddaughters in Dallas and know that my life is awesome!

I invite you to savor your life and enjoy all the blessings that are upon you and never, ever take anything for granted...love your life!!

O.ptimism

STARTING TODAY

You can make your life what you want it to be! Life begins today and looks forward to tomorrow. What matters is who you will become from your actions of today. Always look ahead and leave your pain behind you because you are the designer of your own future.

I remember the time that the #1 thing on my bucket list was to be a grandmother. I dreamed of the moments we would share, the places we would go and the memories we would create.

As I reminisce of days past, I remember all the wonderful times my third granddaughter, Peyton, and I shared. We would laugh, play, eat ice cream, and love just being together. As she grows older and we are living miles apart, we aren't able to have those special times together; however, our love and our bond has never wavered and I love her "to the moon and back."

So, starting today, how can you make your life be what you want it to be?

O.ptimism

DO YOU HAVE A DREAM?

Do you believe you can have, do and be anything your heart desires?

God designed you to come out on top. Allow yourself to have the "who would have thought" blessings.

Miracles do happen—activate your faith and let the seed take root.

Never allow anyone to crush your dreams…they are yours and yours alone. It is up to you to allow them to become your reality!

O.ptimism

KEEP YOUR FEET MOVING

If you have a dream, a goal, a purpose or a desire, how are you going to get it if you don't keep your feet moving toward it? Standing still and being in negative energy will get you nothing but hurt, frustration and staleness. We only get to pass this way but once, so why not have all you want and all you deserve? Never allow any challenge that appears in your life to slow you down. Always keep your faith, a positive attitude and let nothing get in your way.

I encourage you to get up every morning with an attitude of gratitude and be thankful that you can keep your feet moving toward the life you dream of!

Never, never quit!!!

O.ptimism

PASSIONATE ABOUT MY LIFE

Life comes in such great abundance. I was in Dallas for the weekend spending quality time with family and friends. Seeing my son and two granddaughters, Peyton and Sidney, brought such joy and made my heart sing!

Our life can be so full of love, laughter, celebration, peace and harmony if we just allow it to be. It is our choice to live in the positive or the negative. We can take the negative out of each situation and learn from that experience. Each one teaches us a life lesson and we grow on our journey.

Lovingly taste each moment as it comes. Take care not to hurry past the richness that is already here. Love your life today.

It is all here now. Live the abundance in your own special way and live your life with passion each and every day!

O.ptimism

EMMIT SMITH SAYS

On Saturday, August 7, 2010, Emmitt Smith of the Dallas Cowboys was inducted into the NFL Hall of Fame. I loved his speech and would like to share parts of it with you because I feel it was not only awesome but some amazing life lessons!

Life's critical principles:

(1) Be of service;

(2) We all need a championship strategy to guide us—to make our dreams come true;

(3) Claim your inner champion—when you do, you will learn to see, hear and feel differently than others; what I most want to convey here is—never, never ever let others define you—you define yourself!

Have a dream—fulfill a mission—write down your goals and how you will fulfill them. It is only a dream until you write it down and then it becomes a goal.

Another critical principle is consistency—it shows value which is necessary for trust, durability and longevity. You have to show up—no matter how tough the game may be, be the best you possibly can be! [3]

No matter if you are a Cowboy fan or not, his words of wisdom have power and truth. "To thine own self be true"—a quote my Mother said over and over to me and my sister. Love your life, dream your dreams and live your life to the fullest!

O.ptimism

REMEMBER

Don't put limits on yourself. So many dreams are waiting to be realized. Decisions are too important to leave to chance. Reach for your peak, your goal, your prize! Dream really, really big and enjoy your life as it unfolds.

There are no limits in your life—only the ones you create for yourself! Touch that fire within you and be excited with your results!

O.ptimism

A NEW LIFE

On August 31, 1999, a new life began for me. As Dr. Crockett spoke the words, "I'm 99% sure you have multiple myeloma," a big glass bubble surrounded me and God spoke to me and I immediately knew I would survive this hurdle. I knew in my heart I had a purpose to live and a mission to accomplish. Within two years, I was free of any cancer!

When you're doing what you know is right, your natural ability to achieve becomes fully engaged. It pulls you successfully through whatever challenges you may encounter.

Nothing can hold you back when the actions necessary to move forward are connected to the very essence of who you are. Feel the real purpose behind what you seek, and you will surely make it so.

I remember hearing my Mama and Daddy say—"where there's a will, there's a way."

O.*ptimism*

FAMILY TIME IS SPECIAL

I think you would agree with me that spending time with family is priceless. I went to Houston this weekend with my son and family for my granddaughter's tennis tournament. The time we spent together was so much fun and nothing that could ever be replaced monetarily. Just the simple pleasures in life sometimes are the absolute best.

Life passes so fast and so furious that we forget to just slow down enough to enjoy simple moments...we always seem to be too tired, too busy, too something that we forget to just be in the moment and love that moment! I got to do that this weekend...my life has been really hectic and I haven't taken time to savor each breath I take.

I am so grateful and blessed to have two loving, devoted sons, two daughter-in-laws who love my sons, and five beautiful, precious granddaughters. God granted me my #1 Bucket List, which I like to call my "Living List!"

O.*ptimism*

CHECK YOUR PRICE TAG

This is a very special day...it is my 4th granddaughter's 4th birthday. Funny thing I realized as I was typing this—4 is my favorite number! Addison is a light in my life—a reminder everyday of how blessed I am to be given life back, to be in perfect health and have the ability to enjoy and savor every moment I spend with her, my other 4 granddaughters, and my entire family as well as friends! God is truly awesome.

This was written in Facebook by a friend and it really got my attention so I want to share it with you...

> *If you're not being treated with love and respect, check your price tag. Perhaps you have marked yourself down. It's YOU who tells people what you're worth by what you accept. Get off the clearance rack and get behind the glass where they keep the valuables! LEARN to value yourself more! If you don't, no one else will!*

> **—Author Unknown**

Wow—very powerful words in that, wouldn't you agree? So many times we value ourselves less and are definitely our own worst enemy. How would life be if we know what a precious jewel we are? Remember—what the mind can conceive, the body will achieve—create your life just the way you want it!

Life is for Laughing, Loving, Forgiving and Living With Passion!

O.*ptimism*

CREATE THE LIFE YOU WANT

ISN'T LIFE FULL OF SURPRISES?? We wake each morning in anticipation of what the new day will bring...What I have learned from my life's journey is that each day is to be celebrated and each moment is to be a grateful experience! Our thoughts and words create our reality so wouldn't it be wise to think and speak only positive things? God gave us the gift of life and the ability to choose our daily experiences. We have options and I invite you to choose wisely.

My 2nd granddaughter, Brooke, just celebrated her birthday. She is such a beautiful, strong minded little girl. She definitely inherited many of her Mamaw's traits. She is determined, hard headed in a good way, and we love so many of the same things, such as owls, crystals, bling and blitz! This precious girl will create the exact life she wants and deserves, there is no doubt about that!

Create the life you want and deserve and wake each morning with an "attitude of gratitude!"

O.ptimism

NOW

NOW is filled with everything that there is. And it is more than you could ever imagine. Please take time each day to experience the miracle of awareness. Choose the direction that you know is yours. To be here in this moment, to be present in this place, is indeed a miracle in itself.

I invite you to be assured that your life's path is your decision. Discover your purpose and follow your dreams. It is yours now. You do not have to wait, as I did, to be reminded just how special you are!

O.ptimism

LIFE'S LITTLE INSTRUCTIONS

Sing in the shower

Treat everyone you meet like you want to be treated

Never refuse homemade brownies

Strive for excellence, not perfection

Compliment 3 people every day

Leave everything a little better than you found it

Keep it simple

Think big thoughts but relish small pleasures

Become the most positive and enthusiastic person you know

Be forgiving of yourself and others

Say "thank you" and "please" a lot

Avoid negative people

Remember other's birthdays

Commit yourself to constant improvement

Look people in the eye

Make new friends but always cherish your old ones

Live your life as an exclamation, not an explanation

Live your dreams believing in miracles

—Author Unknown

Life is brief and very fragile, do that which makes you happy... live your life being grateful for every beautiful moment you have been blessed with!

O.*ptimism*

BEGINNING TODAY

You have a chance to be as happy as
any one person has ever been.
You have an opportunity to be as proud
as anyone you've ever known.
You have the potential to make a very
special dream come true.

And all you have to do...
is recognize the possibilities, the power,
and the wonder of...today.

Yesterday is over and done, so let's
take that out of the equation.
And tomorrow isn't here yet.
Whatever it may bring is surrounded by
more speculation than anything,
so let's take that out of the equation too.
Then do the math:
what we're left with is the perfectly exquisite gift of...***today***.
It's right here, right now, and it hopes
and prays we will do the
right thing by recognizing it for the golden opportunity...
and the gift...that it is.

Living life a day at a time means living
a life that is blessed with

awareness, appreciation, and accomplishment.
For one day, you can be everything you were meant to be.

For one amazing day...

The weight is lifted. The path is clearer.
The goal is attainable. The prayer is
heard. The strength is sure.
The courage is complete. The belief is steady, sweet and true.

For one remarkable day...

There is a brighter light in your life. The
will to walk up the mountain
takes you exactly where you want to go.
The heart understands what serenity really means.
And your hopes and wishes and dreams
will not disappear from view.

For one magnificent day...

—Author Unknown

O.ptimism

KEEP EVERYTHING IN PERSPECTIVE

At some point in our life, we will experience waves of glory and success, as well as major challenges.

Everyone has their day when they can do no wrong and everyone suffers defeat sometimes, but life wouldn't be exciting if there were no challenges nor would there be any reason to focus or anything to learn.

The wonderment of being a child dreaming of the day I would try out for cheerleader began at age six. Many years of observing our high school cheerleaders at the edge of the stands, I was very focused on that special day.

When that awaited day arrived to try out for junior high cheerleader, I had high fever and the mumps. This might be the first time I realized how much your determination can affect your results...I won!

I was determined to keep everything in perspective and not lose sight of my dream of becoming a cheerleader! Are you willing to keep everything in your life in perspective?

O.ptimism

STAYING POSITIVE THROUGH HOME ROBBERY

I have been sending positive messages to you since 2001—well, now I am truly being tested on keeping a positive attitude myself!

I traveled to Katy this past week for our basketball tournament and my home was robbed on Wednesday during the day. They took several things, including some personal identity items, which is a very scary thing! But most of what they took can be replaced. However, the things that cannot be replaced were several of my parent's and grandparent's items that had special meaning and memories. One of my most precious gifts was taken—an engraved gold bracelet my Daddy gave me my first Christmas and my Grandpa's old marbles.

I am so thankful I was not home and no one was harmed, but the anger, violation and invasion I feel just can't be described. I am working very hard and am determined to keep that positive attitude and stay inspired to just move on.

Times are very scary today—so many people are out of jobs and so desperate for money. I feel sorry for them and invite you to pray for them and secure your home and property so that you may never, ever experience this horrible situation.

Savor and celebrate each day as your gift of life and never take anything for granted!!

O.ptimism

SUCCESS

Success does not come to those who merely have great ideas...
Success comes to those who have great ideas
and who follow through on them.

—Author Unknown

What should you follow through on this week to be successful? Why not be like Nike and "Just Do It"...anything your heart desires!

Success is like a treasure. You can never find it until you decide to look for it and dig deep enough to uncover it. Have you found at least one hidden treasure in yourself today? Your life is one big treasure chest—just waiting to be opened and celebrated.

O.ptimism

WHAT IS YOUR VISION?

A new year has begun...do you have a new vision for your year?

We make New Year's resolutions, just to be broken, right? Well, why not make it different this year? Dig deep for your dreams and desires.

Do you really, really want these and if so, how much? I know for an absolute fact that if you want something enough, you can have that. "How?" you may ask...

For me, when I have a goal to attain, I write it down and post it in all the places that are visible at all times. That way I can visualize it, think it, feel it, live it and then it is mine! Why not shoot for the moon and even if you miss you will land among the stars. In other words, you will accomplish more than you ever have before. You must keep your faith, set your goals/dreams, and then be like Nike and Just Do It!

Believe in your heart that miracles do happen every single day. Live the life you want and deserve...

O.ptimism

H.O.P.E. IS THE ANCHOR

H.O.P.E. is the anchor of the soul. We can put our anchor into doubt and despair or we can put it in H.O.P.E. (health, optimism, passion, enthusiasm).

To attain permanent H.O.P.E., think about filling your mind with positive thoughts so that you may realize the fullness of all the good that belongs to you by your Divine right. Add the feeling of happiness and joy and you have an abundance of lasting H.O.P.E.!

Most importantly...

Live with no regrets, treat people the way you want to be treated, work like you don't need the money, love with all your heart, sing in the rain, laugh often and live your life in abundance and peace.

CHAPTER 3

H. EALTH
O. PTIMISM
P. ASSION
E. NTHUSIASM

PASSION

Passion is one of my favorite words. I am known for always saying "Live Your Life With Passion." What does that mean to you? Personally when I hear or see the word "passion," it stirs compelling emotions inside me. Being the optimistic person I am, I do my very best to focus on positive emotions—love, joy, happiness, and peace.

Along my life's path, there have been many hurdles to jump and I realized the only way to conquer them is with faith, passion, determination, persistence and perseverance. That has served me well my entire lifetime! With these challenges I have definitely had to continue renewing my passion.

There are many things in life that will catch your eye...

But only a few that will catch your heart...

Pursue Those!

There are NO limits—Touch the fire within.

—Sue

P.assion

LIFE IS AN ECHO

Life is an echo...

What you send out comes back to you.

One today is worth two tomorrows.

Some things have to be believed to be seen.

—Author Unknown

When I read "one today is worth two tomorrows" I remember all the special times I had with my cousin and best friend, Resa. We created so many beautiful memories and on October 18, 1990, she was brutally murdered. That was truly a very difficult hurdle to jump. It was senseless, unnecessary and a very hard thing to accept!

We sometimes take life for granted, never slowing down to savor each precious moment we are given. Please slow down today and enjoy all the glory and blessings that surround you.

P.assion

BE HAPPY

Remember these simple rules to be happy:

- Free your heart from hatred,

- Free your mind from worries,

- Live with passion,

- Give more to others,

- Laugh more often,

- Celebrate every day you are given the gift of life,

- Dream big and expect miracles.

P.assion

FOR ANYONE WHO HAS A DREAM

You can be all of the things you dream of being, if you are willing to work at them and believe in yourself more.

Learn from the mistakes of others—accept them and forgive them.

Take control, and live your own life.

Continue the journey you have begun—the journey inside yourself.

Take strength from those you love, and let those who love you help.

Believe in your own goodness, and then do good things.

Work at being the you that you want to be because you are a wonderful person.

Be thankful for all the potential that you are blessed with.

Everything else will follow and your dreams will come true!

If you have a dream—dream big.

Pursue it with a passion.

The adventure you are ready for is the one you get...

Life is short—go for it!!!

—Jeff Probst—Emmy Night [4]

P.assion

THE BEST IS YET TO COME

We just celebrated a new year's beginning. You have the opportunity to choose your life for the new year. Are you going to make it the best yet or allow the past to control you? That is the easy path but does not have to be the only path!

Every day we must go the extra mile to tear down any wall that we discover within ourselves. Old prejudices, old belief patterns, even our ways of thinking and moment to moment living must be torn down if it does not serve the positive, God-given life we deserve. In this New Year, we must not have any blocks within ourselves, or between other people. Move forward and live the life you so want and deserve because it is yours for the taking!

HAPPY NEW YEAR and may it be your best ever!

P.assion

A DREAM WITHOUT A PLAN IS ONLY A WISH

Do you have a dream?
Do you have a written plan?
Do you believe your dream can become your reality?

In 2006 God gave me the message to write a book. Needless to say, I did everything possible to ignore His message for several years. I did not view myself as a "writer" so it was easy to just say no to writing that book. Over the years the book began to unfold and today you are reading God's messages from my *Good Monday Morning* emails. Of the three questions above, my challenge was to believe my dream could become a reality!

Take action today and love your journey because when your dream becomes alive and real, it will be time to wish upon another dream. Never, ever be without one because they give your life meaning and purpose. Remember to live your life with passion as your dreams unfold. Your life will be remembered as to how you lived it "in the dash," which is the time from the day you were born until the day you go home.

P.assion

HAPPINESS CAN BE SO SIMPLE

I went to Dallas over the weekend and had a wonderful experience of just how simple pure happiness can be. My two granddaughters, Peyton and Sidney went to the mall for lunch and a girl's shopping spree. Of course, after lunch the first store to go in was the Disney store. Sidney had her heart set on buying the exact right thing with her gift certificate.

At age 4, she already has the strong mind and knows exactly what she wants and doesn't want. She immediately picked up a stuffed animal which wasn't the cutest one in the store. Peyton and I encouraged her to look at others, but she had that little guy in a grip and was not about to let it go. Peyton continued to show her other things but Sidney's mind was made up. Peyton finally gave up and said to me, "Mamaw it's gonna be that one for sure, so let's go!"

I stood there observing their interactions and the love and respect they have for each other. It warmed my heart to see that childlike wonderment in full action.

Lesson I learned again that day was "life is full of so many simple things that bring happiness and joy to our hearts, we just need to slow down and accept them!"

P.assion

COMPLETING THINGS

Isn't life about completing things? Whatever that may be, there is such a grand satisfaction when you complete something. I moved to another house a month ago. I have all the "big" stuff done; however, it's those "little" less functional tasks that just keep staring you in the face and you say "I will get that done as soon as I can" but you seem to move on to another project. I am speaking of the clothes in the closet that need to be organized from the day you moved in and they were placed in a random order, the last few minute family pictures to hang, the window coverings, and the office closet! Well, I got that all done this weekend and I am one happy gal!

I realized when I finished all those tasks yesterday afternoon, that I felt such a feeling of relief, excitement and accomplishment...

Life is filled with those little "tasks" that we tend to put off until another time. I realized through my experience this past weekend that if we would tackle them, rather than procrastinate, what a warm fuzzy we would have and that would enable us to move on and create a life filled with fun, love and laughter! Of course, we know that there are always those little tasks to complete, but doesn't that make life more fun when we can check them off our list?

I'm not quite sure why I am sharing all this with you today, but God seems to be putting the words on this page for a reason. I hope it resonates in some way with you.

May today be the first day of the rest of your life...live it with passion and savor every moment with celebration!

P.assion

LIFE MAP

Many of us have roadmaps we envision for the courses we think our lives should take. It's important to get headed in the right direction, but don't get so caught up in the concerns over your destination that you forget to delight in the scenery of each new day.

Remember that some of the secret joys of living are not found by rushing from point A to point B, but by inventing some imaginary letters along the way!

Create your life map the way you want it to be—dream big, create your own reality...it's YOUR life, take ownership of it!

P.assion

YOUR PASSIONATE PURPOSE

Each individual has a unique purpose. People only begin to fulfill their creative potential when they have a high degree of alignment in their lives—that is, when their pursuits and conscious goals are in line with their own purpose.

- What is my life about?

- What do I value?

- What do I treasure?

- What is really important?

- What do I do in my life that is worthwhile?

Have you asked yourself these questions? If yes, respect your answers. If no, please do so, as that will create peace and harmony in your life.

P.assion

ISN'T LIFE JUST GRAND

Isn't life just grand? Every day can be so full of surprises and wonderment. I have had such an incredible last two weeks. I finally was done with apartment living and have moved to a darling house. It is so peaceful and serene. Surrounded by trees and when nature is close it simply is amazing.

My wish for you is that whatever surprises your life brings each day, you will celebrate them and savor every moment. Even the challenges we go through can prove to be our best moments. Every day holds a life lesson—our responsibility is to recognize them and learn from each and every one.

So, today I want to inspire you to live it with passion and commit to make a difference in someone's life. Sometimes just a smile can change someone's attitude!

Life is for Laughing, Loving, Forgiving and Living with Passion!

P.assion

PASSION

Wow—when I turned my desk calendar to October the first page was "PASSION," which I am sure after all these years you know is my favorite word.

When you discover your passion, pursue it and celebrate it. Don't let anyone steal your dreams because with faith, determination, positive attitude and perseverance you can create anything your heart desires! I am living proof of this statement in more than one way!

When we find something we care about more than ourselves, we create passion!

P.assion

THE POWER IS YOURS

You have the power to achieve the best. Allow it.

You have a purpose that comes directly from your authentic essence. Accept it, acknowledge it, explore it, and allow it to flow into every corner of your world.

Striving and fighting only hold you back. Now it is time to live every moment with the positive power you know you have.

Now is the time to love and to fulfill the beauty that you know can be. Now you can let authentic life flow.

The problems hold you back only because you see them as problems. Now it is time to see every circumstance as the opportunity that it is.

Every desire, every hope, every longing is already fulfilled by your possibilities. Now is the time to live them fully.

P.assion

ASPIRE

There are so many "aha's" in Kevin Hall's book, "Aspire," that I feel compelled to share with you. I do so in hopes they will touch your heart as they have mine.

It is our duty to discover our God given talents. Our deepest fear is not that we are inadequate. Our deepest fear is that we are powerful beyond measure.

A talent wasted is a sin. We all have certain talents we've been given. Before we can salute the greatness in others, we must salute the greatness in ourselves. [5]

Does any of this speak to you? I invite you to begin today loving yourself and discover your God given talents – they are there and they are powerful!

P.assion

A GOOD ENOUGH REASON

Allow yourself to want what you really want. Then allow yourself to be driven by that desire. Every possibility is open to you. Connect to the positive and compelling things that won't leave you alone until you make it happen.

Make yourself an offer that you can't refuse. Give yourself a reason that you cannot resist.

Give yourself a good enough reason and you can get yourself to do whatever must be done. Give yourself a meaningful enough reason "WHY," and it will happen.

P.assion

LIFE'S GIFT

Every day we wake, we are blessed with the gift of life—another day, another night, water, the sun, the moon, being with our loved ones. We have the chance to laugh, sing, dance or whatever our hearts desire to do that day. These precious gifts cannot be purchased with money.

I personally have been blessed with many of life's gifts. Just to list a few of the miracle moments in my journey are being voted Junior High Cheerleader, in spite of the fact that I had 103° fever with the mumps, assisted the Dean of Women to create a sorority on my college campus, giving birth at age 20 and 24 to my two bundles of joy, Chip and Brooks, spending loving, fun and memorable times with my cousin, Resa, who was brutally murdered in 1990, healing naturally from an incurable cancer within two years and being blessed with 5 beautiful granddaughters who are the light of my life! What are your life's gifts?

Celebrate your life every day. Be grateful you are given the opportunity to live your life the way you choose—you can dream big and believe in miracles...they do happen!

Each day think positive thoughts that become your reality and choose to live a magical life!

P.assion

BEST DAY EVER

I am sharing with you this week about the most awesome day ever. Yesterday I was invited to go with my daughter in law, Michelle and three granddaughters, Ryan, Brooke and Addison to Hunt, Texas, just past Kerrville. Their friends have a house on the river. We spent the day playing in the water, in canoes and kayaks. It was a perfect day, except we missed Brooks, my son, who was out of town on business.

Addison, my five year old (almost six) granddaughter and I brought home a river rock to remember our fun time. She asked me to write on her rock and before I could even ask what she wanted on it, she said "Mamaw put 'the best day ever.'" That touched my heart deeply! After writing that and the date, she then said, "Mamaw, it needs a heart around it." Then she lovingly placed it in the flowerbed in her back yard. So naturally, I wrote the same thing on my rock and it's on my patio as a token to always remember. Sometimes it's the smallest things that touch the heart so deeply!

It also was another day to remind me how blessed I am. I was able to play in the water with the girls, climbing up and down the ladder, get into the canoe and walk along algae-slippery water to reach the ponds for the girls to play in. Now, that does seem like quite simple tasks; however, in times past I would have never attempted to do because I wasn't physically able to! Today I am and it is those simple pleasures in life that we automatically take for granted we need to be aware of and be thankful for.

We can all learn from a child that there are no boundaries to love and enjoying life. The wonderment of a child is priceless and the beauty of our own life is to never be taken for granted.

P.assion

WHERE ARE YOU?

I continue to hear that we live in one of two states of mind—fear or Faith!

In fear we are insecure, scared, unsafe, timid, and afraid.

In Faith, we are strong, secure, confident, happy and our authentic self...

So, my question to you this Monday morning, is where do you live?

In fear or Faith?

I invite you to live in Faith each and every day, knowing that you are exactly where you are intended to be at this exact time of your life. Never be afraid to be your true self, living your true destiny. Be confident, secure and live your gifted life with passion!

Choose a positive acronym for fear—F E A R

FEEL EXCITED AND READY

P.assion

ATTITUDE VS TALENT

How much does the role of attitude and synergy play into succeeding? Do you think it is possible to have excellent talent but not succeed? I do! I am basing my message to you today on a basketball game that I recently attended.

I experienced a game where the players had more talent than any team in their league; however, their mindset sometimes played havoc on their game. In this particular game I am referencing, I watched very carefully the synergy between the players, coaches and fans. It was dynamic. There was never a doubt they would win the game—not just win the game, but be in control the entire time. However, I have watched this team and seen the opposite—no synergy and negative attitudes with no fire in them. Yes, they lost those games!

So, my message this morning is simply to invite you to always focus on having a positive attitude, have the fire within you to succeed and live in gratitude for your gift of life.

P.assion

MAMA'S INSPIRING WORDS

We just celebrated Mother's Day—a very special time for us to remember that wonderful person who gave us life.

I can still remember some of the lessons my Mama always said to me:

- *Beauty is as beauty does.*

- *To thine own self be true.*

- *You can be or do anything you want if you pull up your boot straps, always keep your faith, and believe and know you can.*

- *Take time along life's journey to stop and smell the roses.*

- *Always keep a song in your heart and dance to it.*

HAPPY MOTHER'S DAY to all the Mothers and Grandmothers...

May you be appreciated for all you do and your life be filled with fun, love and laughter.

P.assion

COMMITMENT

I attended a seminar this weekend. It was a self-development discovery workshop that was so powerful and eye-opening in realizing our purpose/mission on this earth.

One part left me pondering the idea of commitment. I feel sometimes it is viewed as "entrapment." The fact is that we must commit 100% to attain our goals. Think about that— very powerful and very true! You can judge your intentions by your results!

Another way to think about it: "Commitment is doing the things you said you'd do long after the mood has left you."—Jim Parry

Thoughts to ponder on this beautiful day.

P.assion

INNER CONVERSATIONS

What kind of conversations do you have with yourself? What are you saying to yourself right now? You may say, "I don't talk to myself"—you may not think you do, but you are continually telling yourself all kinds of things. These inner conversations are the thoughts you are thinking, the responses you are making, the attitudes you are accepting and projecting to others. If they are negative, you can change them!

I vividly recall in the beginning days of the cancer journey when my pain level was at the highest, every time I passed a mirror I would look myself in the eyes and say out loud ***"I am whole in body, mind and spirit, all is well in my world."*** Those words became my daily mantra and within two months my healing began and my world became a beautiful place again. My inner and outer conversations became my truth and the cancer was gone in two years, whereby the medical journals stated I could have been dead in three to five years!

You change your life by changing the way you think and feel. You do this, day by day, thought by thought, as you watch the conversations you have with yourself. When you replace negative, fearful thoughts with positive, healing, powerful, spiritual reminders of who you are with God, you raise your thinking.

P.assion

FOUR THINGS FOR SURE

In my opinion, there are definitely four things in this lifetime that truly make a difference in your life:

- Your Faith

- Your Determination

- Your Positive Attitude

- The "Fire" in Your Belly

If these resonate with you in any way, I invite you to examine and act on them immediately. Always remember "this ain't no dress rehearsal"—you only have this moment in time—make sure you are living it to the fullest and with passion!!

P.assion

JUST DO IT

My oldest granddaughter, Ryan, definitely got her Mamaw's genes—

She loves quotes and saves them to her phone. She sent me this one after we went to Austin over the weekend for a tennis tournament. I wanted to share this with you today because I feel we all have been there and need to always remember to "Just Do It!"

"Quit making excuses, putting it off, complaining about it, dreaming about it, whining about it, crying about it, believing you can't. Worrying if you can, waiting until you're older, skinnier, richer, braver, or all around better…Suck it up, hold on tight, say a Prayer, make a plan and 'Just Do It!'"

—Author Unknown

P.assion

REASON, PURPOSE, MASSIVE ACTION PLAN

I am living proof that you will get out of life exactly what you ask for.

You must remember that your brain will go for anything you really want, so be exact! Live your life with RPM—Reason, Purpose, Massive Action. If you are poor in the mind you won't attract rich.

Someone's opinion of you really does not make you who you are. What gives your life a sense of value, what keeps you from attaining your goals, what is a full life to you? Questions to ponder as you live each day with an attitude of gratitude.

CHAPTER 4

H. EALTH
O. PTIMISM
P. ASSION
E. NTHUSIASM

ENTHUSIASM

Enthusiasm means to be inspired. It is a synonym for passion.

To me it simply means to be excited about each and every moment we have to experience life. Is there a better feeling than watching the wonderment of a child? They have no boundaries, no limitations, no negative forces preventing them from being excited and having the expectations of good, positive adventures.

Sometimes it's hard to be enthusiastic, especially when faced with obstacles. I remember the days when it was a challenge to bathe myself, wash and dry my hair and the everyday routine things we take for granted. I remember pushing a grocery cart with one arm, asking help from anyone to get things off the shelf for me!

Today I'm blessed to push a grocery cart with both arms and stay aware of someone who may need a helping hand from me. Just gotta love life and be enthusiastic about every moment!

Life Isn't Then...Life Isn't When...Life Is Now!

—Sue

E.nthusiasm

HABITS

We are all creatures of habit and if you make good habits, good habits will make you. This wisdom has been around since ancient times. Aristotle once said, "We are what we repeatedly do. Excellence, then, is not an act but a habit."

Decide today what you want out of this lifetime! Then make a habit to do the right actions to make it your reality. Please always know that "what the mind can conceive, the body will achieve!" That is a promise...

E.nthusiasm

COUNT YOUR BLESSINGS

Wow—I spent the weekend counting my blessings and being ever so grateful. I attended my 50 year (YES, 50 year!) high school reunion. It was fun to relive so many memories and see friends I haven't seen since we graduated!

The weekend was a celebration of coming together again as well as remembering those we have lost over the years. The memorial to them was beautiful and certainly made me so grateful I wasn't on that video screen.

Life goes by so fast and I sometimes forget how fortunate I am to be alive, in perfect health and have a rich, full, loving life. It takes moments like this weekend to slow down and smell the roses.

I invite you to do the same and take time to realize how fortunate you are and how awesome your life is. If it's not, then know it is up to you to change it. Life is a gift and is not measured by the number of breaths we take, but by the moments that take our breath away!

E.nthusiasm

BOILING POINT

At 211°, water is hot. At 212 °, it boils. That one extra degree makes all the difference. Are you content with just being pretty good?

Or are you ready to go the extra degree and have exactly what you want and deserve?

In the early days of the cancer, my right arm was in a sling because my right humerus bone was deteriorated. I had the option to live in pity as a victim or retrain my brain to be fully functional with my left arm and hand. I even learned to pick up things off the floor with my toes when my back was in severe pain. I have a full understanding and respect for going that extra effort to get what your heart desires!

I know you deserve the best and know you have it in you to accomplish just that. So, what are you waiting for?

Go for it—achieve your dreams—celebrate your life!

Life is meant to be lived with passion…

E.nthusiasm

WHAT IS YOUR WORD?

What one word describes you the best? If you want to stretch, grow and live the best life ever, choose that word. Pretend you have turned to a page in a book and highlighted that one word. Instead of seeing hundreds of words on the page, your attention, and intention, is focused immediately on that single word. What you focus on expands and becomes your reality.

Try it, get your friends and family to do the same and watch what happens in your world!

My one word that immediately comes to mind is "tenacity." If I want something enough, I never quit until I get it. Probably has something to do with the red hair!

E.nthusiasm

SAY WHAT YOU MEAN

Remember to always say what you mean.

If you love someone, tell them.

Don't be afraid to express yourself.

Reach out and tell someone what they mean to you.

Because when you decide that it is the right time, it may be too late.

You have the gift of nothing but the best. Sometimes we are conditioned to expect less than the best and to settle for less than the best in life. Releasing the old, speaking words for new good, and picturing it are specific ways for opening your mind to receive. "Good, Better, Best—I will never let it rest, until my Good is Better, and my Better is Best!"

Seize the day.

Never have regrets...

And most importantly, stay close to your family and friends, for they have helped make you the person that you are today—

Love Your Life...Be Enthusiastic About Your Life!

E.nthusiasm

DO YOU?

- Live your life everyday as you desire?

- Love your life as it is?

- Believe you are exactly where you are supposed to be at this exact moment in your life?

- Know that if you think positive thoughts they will create your reality?

- Give thanks and celebrate each day for all your blessings, especially the breath of life?

- Know that you are a miracle and your life can be as you dream it to be?

Doing so, you are living your wonderful life to it's fullest...

E.nthusiasm

FOUR KINDS OF PEOPLE

There are four kinds of people in our lives—those who:

- Add
- Multiply
- Subtract
- Divide

Focus on surrounding yourself with those who add and multiply value to your life. Get in alignment with those who support, love, and encourage you in your everyday lives.

Avoid those who pull you away from your vision, goals and dreams. This is "your" life to live each day, to protect the seeds you plant and to see your vision clearly. Always think BIG, write down your vision and visualize, seeing clearly the outcome.

> *"Ask and it will be given to you; seek and you will find; knock and the door will be opened to you."*

(Matthew 7:7) [6]

My healing process was escalated because of those I chose to be in my life. I surrounded myself with those who loved and believed in me and never doubted I would beat the cancer. I have had many challenges along my life's journey and have chosen to avoid those people with negative energies. It takes so much energy to battle a disease but I never lost sight that with keeping my faith, a positive attitude and determination, I could always win!!

E.nthusiasm

TODAY'S TREASURES

Life comes to you in great abundance.

Lovingly taste each moment as it comes. Take care not to hurry past the richness that is already in your life.

Tomorrow's treasures can wait until tomorrow. Live today's treasures while they are here. I've always loved the quote—

"Yesterday is history, tomorrow is a mystery, but today is the gift."

Give yourself time to absorb the goodness of now. Give yourself time to live with meaning, instead of just rushing through. Make the most of what's now.

For my 16th birthday, my Mama gave me a pillar candle which I thought very strange. Holly Hobby was bending over smelling flowers and the saying on it was "Stop and Smell the Roses." I didn't get it at all...until in my later years when I totally understood the true meaning of that candle. That gift has served me well and I always do my best to slow down and smell the roses of life.

Live the abundance in your own special way.

E.nthusiasm

STEP OUT

Would you agree that if you play it safe in life, you've possibly decided that you don't want to grow anymore?

Step out of your comfort zone and take chances. Look for opportunities that will expand your knowledge, your character and your talents.

The world is full of opportunities that will enhance your life…you just have to grasp them!

E.nthusiasm

ATTITUDE IS EVERYTHING

Live Simply,
Love Generously,
Care deeply,
Speak kindly.... .
Life isn't about waiting for the storm to pass—
It's about learning to dance in the rain!

> *In everyone's life, at some time, our inner fire goes
> out. It is then burst into flame by an encounter with
> another human being. We should all be thankful
> for those who rekindle the inner spirit".*

—Albert Schweitzer [7]

How awesome are those words? Our attitude creates 99% of
our reality in life! So, knowing that, why not dance, dance,
dance?

E.nthusiasm

MAKE YOUR SHOTS

My message today is going to be very short and sweet...My sister gave me this wonderful plaque for Christmas. It says:

YOU MISS 100% OF THE SHOTS YOU NEVER TAKE

Whoa...think about that little statement!!

How many times a day do we not take the shot? Well, it's time to pull up the ole boot straps and take those shots. Life is waiting for you!!

Live your dream, laugh out loud and savor every precious moment you are blessed with.

E.nthusiasm

BEGIN

Begin today to live without limitations. Know that there is always a way to get beyond anything you think is holding you back.

Take those feelings of regret for what you have not done and turn them into passion for what you are able to do. This moment is yours and you can create anything you choose.

Stop repeating to yourself the reasons why you can't...

Begin reminding yourself of all the powerful and meaningful reasons why you must! Your thoughts do become your reality!

In life there are always moments of uncertainty, injustice and unfairness. Yet in each and every turn of events, there is opportunity for achievement, fulfillment and genuine greatness.

Begin today to accept every rich detail of life and know you can transform those details into outstanding successes. Listen to the gentle, genuine voice inside you that knows how beautiful life is.

Delight in the rich rewards that your life's passion creates. Begin today...because you know you can!

May your greatest achievements be in front of you and may you always finish strong. Live each moment creating an abundant, happy, healthy, prosperous, joyful and magical life for yourself.

130

E.nthusiasm

HAPPINESS IS YOUR CHOICE

Don't let your happiness be held hostage. It is always yours to choose, to live, to experience.

You don't need anyone else's permission to be happy. Your life is magnificent not because someone says it is, but because you choose to accept it as such.

Stop seeking to arrange circumstances that will make you happy. Simply choose to be happy, and your circumstances start to line-up and are congruent with that happiness.

Happiness is *your* choice. Choose it any time you wish and begin to live the life you want and deserve!

Make today a very special, blessed day with an abundance of love, fun and laughter...

E.nthusiasm

HONOR THE BEGINNING

Beginnings can be delicate or explosive. They can start almost invisibly or arrive with a big bang.

Beginnings hold the promise of new lessons to be learned, new territory to be explored, and old lessons to be recalled, practiced, and appreciated. Beginnings hold ambiguity, promise, fear and hope.

Don't let the lessons, the experiences of the past, dampen your enthusiasm for beginnings. Just because it's been hard doesn't mean it will always be that difficult. Don't let the heartbreaks of the past cause you to become cynical, or close yourself off to life's magic and promise. Open yourself wide to all that the universe has to say.

Let yourself begin anew. Pack your bags. Choose carefully what you bring, because packing is an important ritual. Take along some humility and the lessons of the past. Toss in some curiosity and excitement about what you haven't yet learned. Say your good-byes to those you're leaving behind. Don't worry who you will meet or where you will go. The way has been prepared. The people you are to meet will be expecting you. A new journey has begun. Let it be magical. Let it unfold!

—Melody Beattie [8]

These words describe so many facets of my life as I'm sure yours. I invite you to read this several times until you truly resonate with it!

All parts of the journey are sacred and holy.

Take time now to honor the beginning.

E.nthusiasm

POSSIBILITIES VS INADEQUACIES

The greatest use of your life is to live your life that the use of your life will out live your life.

—Author Unknown

Now, that's something to think about, huh? You may want to read that over and over until it truly makes sense. It's definitely a tongue twister that is full of truth! The reality is that we can allow our fears and inadequacies to paralyze us or allow them to strengthen us to accomplish endless possibilities. We have a choice—let them allow us to make excuses in our lives or lead others and believe in ourselves!

Which life do you choose—it is yours for the taking—I say "go for it!"

I've been reminded many times in my life of the quote: *"Our deepest fear is not that we are inadequate, but our deepest fear is that we are powerful beyond measure."*

That can surely hold one back from greatness! Focus on your strengths and live the life you deserve...

E.nthusiasm

I CAN DO ANYTHING

I can do anything I set my mind to.
I can make dreams happen by the things I do.
Thinking positively no matter what.
Today and everyday.
For it's all in how I look at things and what's put into play.

I can do anything
In this journey called life:
Laugh, Live, Celebrate...
Soar to new heights, for the world seems a better place when I
seize each new day and as
I journey I'll remember:
"Happiness comes most to those who give it away."

So I'll look forward to each adventure, and listen to my heart,
follow my goals and do my part.
Taking joy in today for it's mine to explore.
For I can do anything
When I let my dreams soar.

—Author Unknown

YES...YES...YES!

E.nthusiasm

THE WAIT IS OVER

The wait is over. This moment is here and it is time to live.

Whatever could have been or should have been, doesn't matter.

Live it fully and richly, as if this is the only time there has ever been and the only time that will ever be. This is not a time for regret or blame or putting off until later. This is your time to live. Feel how exquisitely amazing it is to be, and give the best of yourself now.

You can stop giving energy to your limitations at this very moment.

Give your energy to joy and creation and authentic expression.

The most important time in your life is right now. Live it like it really matters, because it absolutely does.

E.nthusiasm

ISN'T LIFE FULL OF SURPRISES?

Isn't life full of awesome surprises? Every day we wake, we are given the gift of a new beginning. It is up to us as to how we spend that day. We can celebrate and savor each and every moment or stay in a negative rut. Boy, staying in that rut is no fun, is it? Well, the good news is that this morning only YOU can get you out of that rut!

That's right—I invite you to begin this very moment to think only positive thoughts, speak only positive words and manifest the perfect life you desire...you will love the results! And you deserve the best!

E.nthusiasm

EXPLORE NEW POSSIBILITIES

There are always plenty of possibilities, with new ones being born every moment. On a regular basis, pick a new possibility and explore it fully.

Turn down a road you've never traveled before, and find out what's there. Be curious, and let your curiosity lead you in the direction of new discoveries.

As I reflect to my past experiences, I realize the roads taken created my life's lessons. Some were challenging, not so fun, yet most were wonderful. I know now that the hardest ones have created who I am today!

Inject some fresh, new experiences into your life. Challenge yourself and add richness to your life by stepping outside your regular routine.

Surprise your senses with things you've never experienced before. Wake up your spirit by uncovering previously hidden treasures in your world.

Add to life's list of joys. Give new depth and richness to your perspective.

The good things in your life are yours now because there was a time when you chose to find them. Explore some new possibilities, and there is much new value you can find.

E.nthusiasm

NEVER LET GO OF HOPE

One day you will see
that it all has finally come together.

What you have always wished for
has finally come to be.

You will look back
and laugh at what has passed
and you will ask yourself,
"How did I get through all of that?"

Just never let go of hope.
Just never quit dreaming.
And never let love depart from your life.

—Jancarl Campi [9]

Does this describe your life? This certainly describes Sue Thompson's journey in life! Today I am eternally grateful for the life I've been given and love and appreciate it more and more every day. As I look back, I realize it was all for a specific reason, which is for me to do my best to live my life's purpose. What about you?

E.nthusiasm

DREAM BIG DREAMS

Your most prized possession as a human being is your dream. You are rich when you have dreams.

Have your dreams been lost? Have you given up on them, for some reason, sometime, somewhere? If yes, then get that passion restored. You deserve to have your dreams come true and you can make that a reality by manifesting and being very clear on what you want the outcome to be!

What would it take to get the fire burning in you again? Just go make it happen!

E.nthusiasm

7 RULES TO LIVE BY

I had the privilege to hear Nick Vujiic speak at a convention I attended. Nick was born with no arms or legs and has overcome many obstacles and challenges in his life. He is one of the most sought after motivational speakers and is the most amazing and inspiring guy I have ever had the honor to hear. He shared his perspective on the "7 Rules to Live By"—

Be Thankful—each day is a gift we should cherish and celebrate.

Have Courage—it always takes courage to overcome any obstacle that comes our way, but you can always do your best to overcome anything! Lack of courage can always be overcome with purpose. Be proactive, not reactive—don't be trapped in the "if only."

Be Authentic—keep healthy boundaries and balance in your life and be yourself at all times—in other words, always be your authentic self, just as God created you to be.

Persistence is the Key—plant seeds of encouragement and love to yourself. Say to your self—"if I give up, I'll never get up." *At this moment he lays down on the floor and uses his head to get up—it was so inspiring and moving—there was not a dry eye in the audience.*

Leave A Legacy—who you are matters the most. Stop looking at the wrinkles on your face and love who you are unconditionally.

Never Give Up—your heart will always give you passion.

Dream Big—what is your purpose, your mission? Discover and unfold that and begin to live your life on purpose!

—Nick Vujiic [10]

E.nthusiasm

REMEMBER

Remember to share your magic with the people who share your memories. Have feelings that run very deep. Be in touch with your heart. Be a caring person who plays for keeps.

The secret of life is to make the best of whatever comes along. Make every day fresh and new. Don't ever give up...you may not know success if you stop trying one attempt too soon. Get better in some way, each and every day. We always have room for improvement!

E.nthusiasm

ISN'T LIFE AWESOME?

I love what Forest Gump said—"*Life is like a box of chocolates... you just never know what you are going to get.*"

Each morning we awake and begin our day, it should be in celebration and gratitude. With each challenge, we discover a victory—with each sadness there is always a rainbow—with each tear, there is always a sense of relief followed by laughter. So why not celebrate every moment we are given the gift of life? Why not tell someone you love them? Why not today? You love yourself, why not live today as if it is the first day of the rest of your life?

I am so blessed and grateful to be alive and enjoy time with my precious granddaughters. Today my first born granddaughter and one of my man reasons to be alive, Ryan, won yet another tennis tournament. It is so gratifying and amazing to watch her grow into such an incredible young lady and to share the love and respect we have for each other. There is nothing like it in the world...Thank you God that you allowed me to live and enjoy this experience and to have five beautiful granddaughters whom I love so much!

Please be grateful for your life and find the simple pleasures to savor each day.

END NOTES

1. The Bible, Revised Standard Edition, (Thomas Nelson Publishers, 1952)

2. Taken from a daily email called "The Daily Motivator" by Ralph Marston

3. 2010 NLF Hall of Fame Induction

4. 2008 Emmy Awards on TV

5. Various excerpts, *Aspire*, Kevin Hall, (Bookwise Publishing Company, 2009)

6. Holy Bible New International Version, (Zondervan Publishing House, 1985)

7. Received in an email from a friend - no source was listed

8. *Journey to the Heart*, Melody Beattie, (Harper San Francisco, 2010)

9. Day Starter Quote, online, 4/4/2006

10. Keynote speech at 2011 Melaleuca Convention

ABOUT SUE THOMPSON

Sue Thompson was born a fiery redhead with a temper and determination to match. A native Texan, Sue was taught from an early age to "pull up your bootstraps" and keep on going—a lesson that would serve her well both personally and professionally along her life's journey.

It's been this zeal for life that led Sue to start her career in sales by the seventh grade at The Smart Shop ladies boutique. Over the years, Sue has trained, coached, and developed business teams in a variety of industries, including real estate, title insurance, advertising, retail management, printing and publishing. It was in real estate, however, that Sue found her niche, recruiting and building successful real estate offices with two of the nation's top companies.

Sue's insatiable passion, faith in miracles, and joy for life has propelled her forward at every turn—even in the face of what doctors called an "incurable cancer" as well as many other challenges she has faced along her life's journey.

With the same fierce determination and positive attitude, Sue kept the faith and embarked on a journey of wellness. She nourished herself with healthy foods, a loving support system, excellent supplements, and creating a non-toxic home. Two years later, the cancer was gone to the amazement of a Dallas oncologist, who called her a "walking miracle poster child."

Today, over a decade later, Sue is a wellness coach, speaker, and author living in San Antonio, Texas. Through her book,

H.O.P.E. Talks, she helps inspire and empower others to keep the faith, believe in miracles, and take ownership of their health and life. Because as Sue can attest, with H.O.P.E., everything is possible.

Sue's "Why"

CONTACT THE AUTHOR

Sue Thompson can be contacted at

sue@zeal4life.net

Books can be ordered and Subscribe to
Good Monday Morning messages at

www.zeal4life.net

COMING SOON

Sue's Story

"This Ain't No Dress Rehearsal"

MY OWN INSPIRATIONS

_____

_____

_____

_____

_____

_____

_____

_____

_____

_____

_____

_____

_____

_____

_____

_____

_____

MY OWN INSPIRATIONS

_____

_____

_____

_____

_____

_____

_____

_____

_____

_____

_____

_____

_____

_____

_____

MY OWN INSPIRATIONS

_____

_____

_____

_____

_____

_____

_____

_____

_____

_____

_____

_____

_____

_____

_____

_____

MY OWN INSPIRATIONS

_____

_____

_____

_____

_____

_____

_____

_____

_____

_____

_____

_____

_____

_____

_____

_____

MY OWN INSPIRATIONS

Made in the USA
San Bernardino, CA
03 November 2013